GLOBAL INVESTMENT PERFORMANCE STANDARDS (GIPS®) FOR VERIFIERS

2020

CFA Institute®
Global Investment
Performance Standards

ISBN 978-1-942713-73-9

CONTENTS

PREFACE

CFA Institute is a global not-for-profit association of investment professionals with the mission of leading the investment profession globally by setting the highest standards of ethics, education, and professional excellence. CFA Institute has a longstanding history of commitment to establishing and supporting the Global Investment Performance Standards (GIPS®). The GIPS standards are ethical standards for calculating and presenting investment performance based on the principles of fair representation and full disclosure.

The GIPS standards are the recognized standard for calculating and presenting investment performance around the world. Compliance with the GIPS standards has become a firm's "passport" to market investment management services globally. Asset owners that comply demonstrate a commitment to adhering to global best practices. As of June 2019, CFA Institute has partnered with organizations in more than 40 countries and regions that contribute to the development and promotion of the GIPS standards.

History

- In 1995, CFA Institute, formerly known as the Association for Investment Management and Research (AIMR), sponsored and funded the Global Investment Performance Standards Committee to develop global standards for calculating and presenting investment performance, based on the existing AIMR Performance Presentation Standards (AIMR-PPS®).
- The first Global Investment Performance Standards were published in April 1999. That year, the Global Investment Performance Standards Committee was replaced by the Investment Performance Council (IPC) to further develop and promote the GIPS standards. The development of the GIPS standards was a global industry initiative with participation from individuals and organizations from more than 15 countries.
- The IPC was charged with developing provisions for other asset classes (e.g., real estate and private equity) and addressing other performance-related issues (e.g., fees and advertising) to broaden the scope and applicability of the GIPS standards. The second edition of the GIPS standards, published in February 2005, accomplished this goal.
- With the 2005 edition release and the growing adoption and expansion of the GIPS standards, the IPC decided to move to a single global investment performance standard that would eliminate the need for local variations of the GIPS standards. All country-specific performance standards converged with the GIPS standards, resulting in 25 countries adopting a single, global standard for the calculation and presentation of investment performance.

- In 2005, with the convergence of country-specific versions to the GIPS standards and the need to reorganize the governance structure to facilitate involvement from GIPS Standards Sponsors, CFA Institute dissolved the IPC and created the GIPS Executive Committee and the GIPS Council. The GIPS Executive Committee served as the decision-making authority for the GIPS standards, and the GIPS Council facilitated the involvement of all GIPS Standards Sponsors in the ongoing development and promotion of the GIPS standards.
- In 2008, the GIPS Executive Committee began a review of the GIPS standards in an effort to further refine the provisions. The GIPS Executive Committee collaborated closely with its technical subcommittees, specially formed working groups, and GIPS Standards Sponsors. These groups reviewed the existing provisions and guidance and conducted surveys and other research in the effort to produce the 2010 edition of the GIPS standards.
- In 2017, the GIPS Executive Committee concluded that the GIPS standards should better accommodate the needs of managers of pooled funds and alternative investments, as well as firms focusing on high-net-worth clients. In 2017, a Consultation Paper, which described the proposed key concepts of the GIPS standards and requested feedback on specific issues, was issued for public comment. The public comments received generally supported the proposed concepts. Subsequently, the 2020 GIPS Standards Exposure Draft was released on 31 August 2018. The final version of the 2020 edition of the GIPS standards was issued on 30 June 2019.
- The GIPS standards were originally created for investment firms managing composite strategies, with a focus on how firms present performance of composites to prospective clients. Asset owners, who were always able to claim compliance if they had discretion over their assets, struggled to understand how the GIPS standards applied to them. To address asset owners' needs, in 2014 the Guidance Statement on the Application of the GIPS Standards to Asset Owners was issued. This Guidance Statement explained how the requirements of the GIPS standards did or did not apply to asset owners. In the 2020 edition, separate provisions were created so that firms and asset owners each have provisions designed for them. Firms and those asset owners that market their services must follow the GIPS Standards for Firms. Asset owners that do not market their services will follow the GIPS Standards for Asset Owners. The GIPS Standards for Verifiers explain the procedures a verifier must follow when conducting a verification or performance examination.

INTRODUCTION

Preamble—Why Is a Global Investment Performance Standard Needed?

Standardize Investment Performance: Financial markets and the investment management industry have become increasingly global in nature. The growth in the types and number of financial entities, the globalization of the investment process, and the increased competition among investment management firms all demonstrate the need to standardize the calculation and presentation of investment performance.

Global Passport: Asset managers and both existing and prospective clients benefit from an established global standard for calculating and presenting investment performance. Investment practices, regulation, performance measurement, and reporting of performance vary considerably from country to country. By adhering to a global standard, firms in countries with minimal or no investment performance standards can compete for business on an equal footing with firms from countries with more-developed standards. Firms from countries with established practices can have more confidence in being fairly compared with local firms when competing for business in countries that have not previously adopted performance standards. Performance standards that are accepted globally enable investment firms to measure and present their investment performance so that investors can readily compare investment performance among firms.

Investor Confidence: Organizations that adhere to investment performance standards help assure investors and beneficiaries that the firm's and the asset owner's investment performance is complete and fairly presented. Both prospective and existing clients of investment firms as well as asset owner oversight bodies benefit from a global investment performance standard by having a greater degree of confidence in the performance information presented to them.

Mission and Objectives

The mission of the GIPS standards is to promote ethics and integrity and instill trust through the use of the GIPS standards by achieving universal demand for compliance by asset owners, adoption by asset managers, and support from regulators for the ultimate benefit of the global investment community.

The objectives of the GIPS standards are as follows:

- Promote investor interests and instill investor confidence.
- Ensure accurate and consistent data.

- Obtain worldwide acceptance of a single standard for calculating and presenting performance.
- Promote fair, global competition among investment firms.
- Promote industry self-regulation on a global basis.

Overview

Key concepts of the GIPS standards that apply to verifiers include the following:

- The GIPS standards recommend that firms and asset owners be verified. Verification is a process by which a verification firm (verifier) conducts testing of a firm on a firm-wide basis, or an asset owner on an asset owner–wide basis, in accordance with the required verification procedures of the GIPS standards. Verification provides assurance on whether the firm's or asset owner's policies and procedures related to total fund, composite, and pooled fund maintenance, as well as the calculation, presentation, and distribution of performance, have been designed in compliance with the GIPS standards and have been implemented on a firm-wide or asset owner–wide basis.
- The verifier must be independent from the firm or asset owner. To be independent, there must be no independence issues between the verifier and the firm or asset owner. The verifier must perform its service in an unbiased manner and must not be testing its own work.
- In addition to being independent, the verifier must be qualified. To be qualified, a verifier must have certain attributes, including having appropriate professional abilities and experience as well as a practical level of expertise regarding audit methodology and investment management practices. The verifier must also be knowledgeable about the GIPS standards as well as applicable laws and regulations regarding the calculation and presentation of performance.
- A verifier must conduct the verification in accordance with the required verification procedures of the GIPS standards. These are the minimum procedures that the verifier must perform when conducting a verification.
- Firms and asset owners may also choose to have specifically focused testing of a composite, pooled fund, or total fund (performance examination) performed by an independent third-party verifier to provide additional assurance regarding a particular composite, pooled fund, or total fund. A verifier must conduct the performance examination in accordance with the required performance examination procedures of the GIPS standards. These are the minimum procedures that the verifier must perform when conducting a performance examination.

Effective Date

The effective date for the 2020 edition of the GIPS standards is 1 January 2020. GIPS Reports and GIPS Asset Owner Reports that include performance for periods ending on or after 31 December 2020 must be prepared in accordance with the 2020 edition of the GIPS standards. Prior editions of the GIPS standards may be found on the CFA Institute website (www.cfainstitute.org).

Firms and asset owners may early adopt the 2020 edition of the GIPS standards. Verifiers must conduct their verification and performance examination engagements in accordance with the 2020 edition of the GIPS Standards for Verifiers for periods for which the firm or asset owner claims compliance following the 2020 edition of the GIPS standards. Verifiers are recommended to conduct their verification and performance examination engagements in accordance with the 2020 edition of the GIPS Standards for Verifiers for all periods for which they are conducting the engagement.

Implementing a Global Standard

One objective of the GIPS standards is to obtain worldwide acceptance of a single standard for the calculation and presentation of investment performance in a fair and comparable format that provides full disclosure. To facilitate the implementation of the GIPS standards, CFA Institute, together with the GIPS standards governing bodies, creates and administers the GIPS standards while local GIPS Standards Sponsors help to promote them.

Countries without an investment performance standard are strongly encouraged to promote the GIPS standards as the local standard and translate them into the local language when necessary. Although the GIPS standards may be translated into many languages, if a discrepancy arises, the English version of the GIPS standards is the official governing version.

The self-regulatory nature of the GIPS standards necessitates a strong commitment to ethical integrity. Self-regulation also assists regulators in exercising their responsibility for ensuring the fair disclosure of information within financial markets. Regulators are encouraged to do the following:

- Recognize the benefit of voluntary compliance with standards that represent global best practices;
- Consider taking enforcement action against firms and asset owners that falsely claim compliance with the GIPS standards; and
- Recognize the value of and encourage independent third-party verification.

Where existing laws, regulations, or industry standards already impose requirements related to the calculation and presentation of investment performance, firms and asset owners are strongly encouraged to comply with the GIPS standards in addition to applicable regulatory requirements. Compliance with applicable laws and regulations does not necessarily lead to compliance with the GIPS standards. In cases in which laws and/or regulations conflict with the GIPS standards, firms and asset owners are required to comply with the laws and regulations and make full disclosure of the conflict in the GIPS Report or GIPS Asset Owner Report.

GIPS Standards Sponsors

The presence of a local GIPS Standards Sponsor is essential for effective implementation of the GIPS standards and ongoing support within a country or region. Working in partnership with CFA Institute, GIPS Standards Sponsors play a key role in promoting the GIPS standards globally. GIPS Standards Sponsors, composed of one or more industry organizations, provide an important link between their local markets and the GIPS standards governing bodies. In addition to delivering educational programs and promoting the GIPS standards across the local investment profession, the GIPS Standards Sponsors own any CFA Institute-approved translation of the GIPS standards materials and are responsible for protecting it.

Endorsed GIPS Standards Sponsors (as of 30 June 2019)

Australia
Financial Services Council (FSC)

Canada
Canadian Investment Performance Council (CIPC)

China
CFA Society Beijing

Cyprus
CFA Society Cyprus

Czech Republic
CFA Society Czech Republic and Czech Capital Market Association (AKAT)

Denmark
CFA Society Denmark and The Danish Finance Society

France
CFA Society France and Association Française de la Gestion Financière (AFG)

Germany
German Asset Management Standards Committee (GAMSC):
Bundesverband Investment und Asset Manager e.V. (BVI); Deutsche Vereinigung fur Finanzanalyse und Assetment Management (DVFA); and CFA Society Germany

Ghana
Ghana Securities Industry Association (GSIA)

Greece
CFA Society Greece

India
CFA Society India

Indonesia
CFA Society Indonesia and Indonesia Association of Mutual Fund Managers (Asosiasi Pengelola Reksa Dana Indonesia, or APRDI)

Ireland
Irish Association of Investment Managers (IAIM)

Italy
Italian Investment Performance Committee (IIPC):
Associazione Bancaria Italiana (ABI); Associazione Italiana degli Analisti e Consulenti Finanziari (AIAF); Assogestioni; Società per lo sviluppo del Mercato dei Fondi Pensione (Mefop); Associazione Italiana Revisori Contabili (Assirevi); and CFA Society Italy

Japan
The Securities Analysts Association of Japan (SAAJ)

Kazakhstan
Association of Financial and Investment Analysts (AFIA)

Korea
Korea Investment Performance Committee (KIPC)

Liechtenstein
Liechtenstein Bankers Association (LBA)

Mexico
CFA Society Mexico

Micronesia
Asia Pacific Association for Fiduciary Studies (APAFS)

The Netherlands
VBA-Beleggingsprofessionals

New Zealand
CFA Society New Zealand

Nigeria
Nigeria Investment Performance Committee: CFA Society Nigeria; Pensions Operators Association of Nigeria (PENOP); and Fund Managers Association of Nigeria (FMAN)

Norway
The Norwegian Society of Financial Analysts (NFF)

Pakistan
CFA Society Pakistan

Peru
Procapitales

Philippines
CFA Society Philippines; Fund Managers Association of the Philippines (FMAP); and Trust Officers Association of the Philippines (TOAP)

Poland
CFA Society Poland

Portugal
Associação Portuguesa de Analista Financeiros (APAF)

Russia
CFA Association Russia

Saudi Arabia
CFA Society Saudi Arabia

Singapore
Investment Management Association of Singapore (IMAS)

South Africa
Association for Savings and Investment South Africa (ASISA)

Spain
Asociación Española de Presentación de Resultados de Gestión

Sri Lanka
CFA Society Sri Lanka

Sweden
CFA Society Sweden and The Swedish Society of Financial Analysts (Sveriges Finansanalytikers Forening, or SFF)

Switzerland
Swiss Funds & Asset Management Association (SFAMA)

Thailand
The Association of Provident Fund (AOP)

Ukraine
The Ukrainian Association of Investment Business (UAIB)

United Kingdom
United Kingdom Investment Performance Committee (UKIPC):
The Investment Association (TIA);
The Association of British Insurers (ABI);
Pensions and Lifetime Savings Association (PLSA); The Association of Consulting Actuaries (ACA); The Society of Pension Consultants (SPC); The Investment Property Forum (IPF); The Alternative Investment Management Association (AIMA); and
The Wealth Management Association (WMA)

United States
United States Investment Performance Committee (USIPC) of CFA Institute

The Global Investment Performance Standards for Verifiers

The 2020 Edition of the GIPS Standards has three chapters:

1) GIPS Standards for Firms
2) GIPS Standards for Asset Owners
3) GIPS Standards for Verifiers

The GIPS Standards for Verifiers is split into two main sections—one for verification and the other for performance examination. These sections include the following topics:

Verification

- Purpose of Verification
- Verifier Qualification Requirements
- Scope of Verification
- Agreeing on the Terms of the Engagement
- Required Verification Procedures
- Maintenance of Verifier Documentation
- Representation Letter
- Verification Report
- Recommendation Letter

Performance Examination

- Purpose and Scope of Performance Examination
- Verifier Qualification Requirements
- Agreeing on the Terms of the Engagement
- Required Performance Examination Procedures
- Maintenance of Verifier Documentation
- Representation Letter
- Performance Examination Report
- Recommendation Letter

The GIPS Standards for Verifiers also include a glossary for defined terms that appear in small capital letters, a sample verification report, and a sample performance examination report.

VERIFICATION

Purpose of Verification

VERIFICATION is intended to provide a FIRM and its prospective and current clients and POOLED FUND investors additional confidence in the FIRM's claim of compliance with the GIPS standards. VERIFICATION may increase the knowledge of the FIRM's performance measurement team and improve the consistency and quality of the FIRM's GIPS standards–related performance information. VERIFICATION may result in improved internal policies and procedures as well as marketing advantages for the FIRM.

The GIPS standards RECOMMEND that FIRMS be verified. VERIFICATION brings additional credibility to the claim of compliance and supports the overall guiding principles of full disclosure and fair representation of a FIRM's investment performance. In defining the minimum REQUIRED VERIFICATION procedures, the GIPS standards governing bodies considered the cost and effort that FIRMS MUST undertake to be verified.

Just as FIRMS may do, ASSET OWNERS may choose to be verified. VERIFICATION is intended to provide an ASSET OWNER and its OVERSIGHT BODY additional confidence in the ASSET OWNER'S claim of compliance with the GIPS standards. The 2020 edition of the GIPS Standards for Verifiers does not include VERIFICATION guidance specific to ASSET OWNERS. When considering this guidance for conducting a VERIFICATION of an ASSET OWNER, verifiers MUST interpret references to FIRMS as also referring to ASSET OWNERS, and they MUST interpret references to COMPOSITES as also referring to TOTAL FUNDS and additional COMPOSITES. Verifiers that conduct VERIFICATIONS for ASSET OWNERS MUST follow the REQUIRED VERIFICATION procedures to the extent possible, and they MUST tailor these procedures to fit the unique facts and circumstances of the ASSET OWNER. Verifiers MUST document their rationale for their testing approach, including why any REQUIRED VERIFICATION procedure was modified or not appropriate.

Verifier Qualification Requirements

The VERIFICATION MUST be performed by a qualified independent third party:

- Verifiers MUST have appropriate professional abilities and experience, as well as a practical level of expertise regarding audit methodology and investment management practices, including investment accounting, performance calculation methodologies, and business processes.
- Verifiers MUST be knowledgeable about the GIPS standards and MUST understand all the REQUIREMENTS and RECOMMENDATIONS of the GIPS standards, including all Guidance

Statements, interpretations, and Questions & Answers (Q&As) published by CFA Institute and the GIPS standards governing bodies.

- Verifiers MUST also be knowledgeable about applicable laws and regulations regarding the calculation and presentation of performance.

The verifier MUST be independent from the FIRM. Please see the Guidance Statement on Verifier Independence for additional guidance.

Verifiers are auditing, consulting, and other firms that have a high degree of knowledge about the investment management industry. Verifiers MUST follow any applicable professional guidance and standards of practice within their industry when conducting a VERIFICATION.

Scope of Verification

A single VERIFICATION REPORT is issued on a FIRM-wide basis. VERIFICATION cannot be carried out only on a COMPOSITE or a POOLED FUND and, accordingly, provides no assurance about the performance of any specific COMPOSITE or POOLED FUND or any specific GIPS REPORT. FIRMS MUST NOT state that a specific COMPOSITE or POOLED FUND has been "verified" or make any claim to that effect.

FIRMS MUST comply with all applicable REQUIREMENTS of the GIPS standards, which include REQUIREMENTS beyond those specified in the REQUIRED VERIFICATION procedures. Therefore, VERIFICATION does not provide assurance on the FIRM's claim of compliance with the GIPS standards in its entirety.

The initial minimum period for which a VERIFICATION can be performed is one year (or from FIRM inception date through period end if less than one year) of a FIRM's presented performance. It is RECOMMENDED that FIRMS be verified for all period(s) for which compliance with the GIPS standards is claimed.

Agreeing on the Terms of the Engagement

Prior to commencing the engagement, the verifier MUST agree on the terms of the VERIFICATION with the FIRM. The agreed terms MUST be specified in an engagement letter or other suitable form of written agreement and MUST include the following:

a. The objective and scope of the engagement, including the period(s) being verified;
b. The verifier's responsibilities;
c. The FIRM's responsibilities;
d. A statement about the inherent limitations of a VERIFICATION;

e. A statement that the GIPS standards are the evaluation criteria for the engagement;

f. A statement that the VERIFICATION does not provide assurance on the operating effectiveness of the FIRM's controls or policies and procedures for complying with the GIPS standards; and

g. A statement that the FIRM agrees to provide the verifier with a representation letter at the conclusion of the VERIFICATION.

The engagement letter SHOULD also include any other terms and conditions relevant to the VERIFICATION.

Required Verification Procedures

A VERIFICATION MUST be conducted in accordance with the REQUIRED VERIFICATION procedures of the GIPS standards. The following are the minimum procedures verifiers MUST perform when conducting a VERIFICATION. Verifiers MUST complete the VERIFICATION in accordance with these procedures prior to issuing a VERIFICATION REPORT to the FIRM.

Planning Procedures

The verifier MUST consider the following presumptions:

- Information obtained from independent third parties provides greater assurance than information obtained from the FIRM;
- Information obtained from the verifier's direct personal knowledge (such as through tangible documentation, observation, computation, operating tests, or inspection) is more persuasive than information obtained indirectly; and
- Information obtained from a FIRM with an effective control environment is more reliable than information obtained from a FIRM without an effective control environment.

The verifier MUST consider the following matters when designing test procedures:

- The nature and materiality of the information to be tested;
- The control environment (including the extent to which automated and manual processes are used);
- The likelihood of misstatements;
- Knowledge obtained during current and previous engagements;
- The extent to which the information is affected by judgment; and
- Inadequacies in the underlying data.

When conducting a VERIFICATION, the verifier MUST accumulate sufficient evidence and perform sufficient procedures such that the risk of not detecting errors during the VERIFICATION is mitigated to an acceptably low level.

Testing by inquiry on its own is insufficient to satisfy the REQUIRED VERIFICATION procedures when other testing procedures could reasonably be performed (e.g., inspection, observation, or recalculation). Verifiers MUST review sufficient and appropriate supporting documentation when conducting VERIFICATION procedures.

A verifier may choose to rely on the audit and/or internal control work of a qualified and reputable independent third party. In addition, a verifier may choose to rely on other audit and/or internal control work it has provided to the FIRM. A verifier may also accept the VERIFICATION work of another verifier as part of the basis for the VERIFICATION REPORT. If the verifier plans to rely on work performed by another party, then the work—including scope, period(s) covered, results of procedures performed, and the other party's qualifications, competency, objectivity, and reputation—MUST be assessed by the verifier when determining whether to place any reliance on such work. Reliance considerations and conclusions MUST be documented by the verifier. The verifier MUST use professional skepticism when deciding whether to place reliance on work performed by another party.

Sample Selection

Verifiers MUST subject the entire FIRM to testing when conducting VERIFICATION procedures. Verifiers may use a sampling methodology when performing such testing procedures. The verifier MUST determine not only the appropriate sample size but also whether the sample selected is reasonable considering the FIRM's specific circumstances. The verifier MUST select samples from the entire period(s) being verified.

Verifiers MUST consider the following criteria when selecting samples:

- Number of COMPOSITES and POOLED FUNDS at the FIRM;
- Number of PORTFOLIOS in each COMPOSITE;
- COMPOSITE DEFINITIONS and POOLED FUND strategies;
- Legal structure of the POOLED FUNDS;
- COMPOSITE assets and POOLED FUND assets relative to TOTAL FIRM ASSETS;
- Internal control environment at the FIRM;
- Number of years being verified;
- Systems used in the construction and maintenance of COMPOSITES;
- Methodology and systems used for calculating and reporting performance; and
- The use of external service providers.

This list is not all-inclusive and contains only the minimum criteria that MUST be considered in the selection and evaluation of a sample. For example, one potentially useful approach would be to include in the sample a PORTFOLIO that has the largest effect on COMPOSITE performance because of its size. Missing or incomplete documents, or the presence of errors, would warrant selecting a larger sample or applying additional VERIFICATION procedures.

Testing Procedures

1. Recordkeeping: While conducting the REQUIRED testing procedures, verifiers MUST determine whether:
    a. The FIRM has captured and maintained the data and information necessary to support all items included in GIPS REPORTS and GIPS ADVERTISEMENTS.
    b. The data and information are available within a reasonable time.
    c. The data and information are sufficient to support the claim of compliance on a FIRM-wide basis.

    Detailed examples of data and information that could be examined are provided in the Guidance Statement on Recordkeeping Requirements.
2. Policies and Procedures: Verifiers MUST obtain the FIRM's policies and procedures used in establishing and maintaining compliance with the GIPS standards. Verifiers MUST understand the FIRM's policies and procedures for establishing and maintaining compliance with all the applicable REQUIREMENTS and adopted RECOMMENDATIONS of the GIPS standards.

    Verifiers MUST perform sufficient procedures to determine that:
    a. The FIRM's policies and procedures are consistent with the GIPS standards;
    b. The FIRM's policies and procedures are complete, clear, unambiguous, and adequately documented; and
    c. The FIRM's policies and procedures are suitably designed to enable the FIRM to comply with the GIPS standards.
3. FIRM Definition: Verifiers MUST gain an understanding of the FIRM, including the corporate structure of the FIRM and how it operates. Verifiers MUST perform sufficient procedures to determine that the FIRM is, and has been, appropriately defined.
4. Lists of COMPOSITES and POOLED FUNDS: Verifiers MUST obtain the FIRM's list of COMPOSITE DESCRIPTIONS, list of POOLED FUND DESCRIPTIONS for LIMITED DISTRIBUTION POOLED FUNDS, and list of BROAD DISTRIBUTION POOLED FUNDS, and then perform sufficient procedures to determine that these lists are complete.
5. TOTAL FIRM ASSETS: For each annual period end within the period(s) being verified, verifiers MUST obtain:
    - A list of all PORTFOLIOS, with each PORTFOLIO's value, that constitute TOTAL FIRM ASSETS;
    - A list of all PORTFOLIOS included in COMPOSITES;

- A list of all SEGREGATED ACCOUNTS that are not included in any COMPOSITE; and
- A list of all POOLED FUNDS that are not included in any COMPOSITE.

Verifiers MUST select PORTFOLIOS from these lists and perform sufficient procedures to determine that:

a. The list of all PORTFOLIOS that constitute TOTAL FIRM ASSETS, with each PORTFOLIO'S value, is complete.

b. PORTFOLIOS included in COMPOSITES and other PORTFOLIOS not included in COMPOSITES are properly included in TOTAL FIRM ASSETS and have not been double-counted.

c. PORTFOLIOS included in TOTAL FIRM ASSETS are properly included in or excluded from COMPOSITES.

d. TOTAL FIRM ASSETS reflect only actual assets managed by the FIRM.

e. TOTAL FIRM ASSETS are calculated accurately and reflect all assets for which the FIRM has investment management responsibility.

6. PORTFOLIOS Excluded from COMPOSITES: Verifiers MUST obtain a list of all PORTFOLIOS that are classified as non-discretionary and excluded from COMPOSITES during the period(s) being verified. Verifiers MUST select PORTFOLIOS from this list and perform sufficient procedures to determine that the FIRM'S classification of the PORTFOLIOS as non-discretionary is appropriate by referring to the PORTFOLIO'S investment mandate, objective, or strategy, as indicated by the PORTFOLIO'S investment management agreement, investment guidelines, and other appropriate documentation.

7. Assignment of PORTFOLIOS to COMPOSITES: Verifiers MUST obtain COMPOSITE membership details, including which PORTFOLIOS are included, with their returns and values, for all period(s) being verified. This information MUST include new, existing, and terminated PORTFOLIOS. Verifiers MUST select PORTFOLIOS from COMPOSITES and perform sufficient procedures to determine that:

a. The FIRM has defined and maintained COMPOSITES in compliance with the GIPS standards.

b. The FIRM'S policies and procedures for creating and maintaining COMPOSITES have been consistently applied.

c. PORTFOLIOS included in COMPOSITES are properly classified as discretionary, as indicated by the PORTFOLIO'S investment management agreement, investment guidelines, and other appropriate documentation.

d. The investment mandate, objective, or strategy of PORTFOLIOS included in COMPOSITES, as indicated by the PORTFOLIO'S investment management agreement, investment guidelines, PORTFOLIO holdings, and other appropriate documentation, is consistent with the COMPOSITE DEFINITION.

e. PORTFOLIOS included in the same COMPOSITE share a similar investment mandate, objective, or strategy.

   f. The timing of inclusion of new PORTFOLIOS in COMPOSITES is in accordance with the FIRM'S new PORTFOLIO policies and procedures.
   g. The timing of exclusion of terminated PORTFOLIOS from COMPOSITES is in accordance with the FIRM'S terminated PORTFOLIO policies and procedures.
   h. Movements of PORTFOLIOS from one COMPOSITE to another are appropriate; consistent with documented changes to a PORTFOLIO'S investment mandate, objective, or strategy or the redefinition of the COMPOSITE; and in accordance with the FIRM'S moved PORTFOLIO policies and procedures.
   i. For COMPOSITES that have a COMPOSITE minimum asset level, and only for those COMPOSITES, PORTFOLIOS are included in and excluded from COMPOSITES in accordance with the FIRM'S minimum asset level policies and procedures.
   j. For COMPOSITES that have a SIGNIFICANT CASH FLOW policy, and only for those COMPOSITES, PORTFOLIOS are included in and excluded from COMPOSITES in accordance with the FIRM'S SIGNIFICANT CASH FLOW policies and procedures.
   k. For COMPOSITES that exclude non-fee-paying PORTFOLIOS, and only for those COMPOSITES, non-fee-paying PORTFOLIOS are excluded from COMPOSITES in accordance with the FIRM'S non-fee-paying PORTFOLIO policies and procedures.
8. Outlier Returns: Verifiers MUST perform sufficient procedures to determine that outlier returns within COMPOSITES do not indicate PORTFOLIO return or COMPOSITE assignment errors. Verifiers MUST:
   a. For a sample of COMPOSITES, review PORTFOLIO returns within the COMPOSITE, to identify PORTFOLIOS with returns that significantly deviate from the returns of other PORTFOLIOS within the COMPOSITE.
   b. Select a sample of PORTFOLIOS with outlier returns and for each PORTFOLIO determine that:
      i. There are no input data or PORTFOLIO return calculation errors relating to the outlier returns.
      ii. The PORTFOLIO is properly included in the COMPOSITE.
9. Input Data: For selected PORTFOLIOS, verifiers MUST perform sufficient procedures to determine that the treatment of the following items is consistent with the FIRM'S policies and procedures:
   a. Classification of PORTFOLIO flows (e.g., receipts, disbursements, dividends, interest, fees, expenses, and taxes);
   b. Accounting treatment of dividend and interest income;
   c. Accounting treatment of taxes, tax reclaims, and tax accruals;
   d. Accounting treatment of TRANSACTION COSTS;
   e. Accounting treatment of fees and expenses; and
   f. Accounting treatment of and valuation methodologies for investments.

10. Performance Based on Actual Assets: For selected PORTFOLIOS, verifiers MUST perform sufficient procedures to determine that PORTFOLIO holdings, income, and cash flows are supported by appropriate documents from independent third parties, if applicable. Examples of appropriate documents include custodian, fund accounting, and broker statements, as well as client subscription and redemption notifications.

11. Performance Measurement: Verifiers MUST perform sufficient procedures to determine that the FIRM has calculated performance in accordance with the REQUIREMENTS of the GIPS standards and the FIRM's policies and procedures. Verifiers MUST, for a sample of PORTFOLIO and COMPOSITE returns, recalculate returns to determine that:

    a. An acceptable return formula as REQUIRED by the GIPS standards is used.

    b. The FIRM's calculations, including the treatment of any fees and expenses, are in accordance with the FIRM's policies and procedures.

12. GIPS REPORTS: Verifiers MUST perform sufficient procedures on a sample of GIPS REPORTS to determine that each GIPS REPORT includes all the numerical information and disclosures REQUIRED by the GIPS standards. If the FIRM includes total FIRM OVERLAY EXPOSURE, total uncalled COMMITTED CAPITAL, total FIRM ADVISORY-ONLY ASSETS, SUPPLEMENTAL INFORMATION, performance from a past firm or affiliation, or custom BENCHMARKS in GIPS REPORTS, verifiers SHOULD include GIPS REPORTS that include such information in this sample.

    For each GIPS REPORT selected for testing, verifiers MUST perform the following procedures:

    a. Test COMPOSITE, POOLED FUND, and BENCHMARK calculations to determine that all presented numerical information, except SUPPLEMENTAL INFORMATION:

        i. Adheres to the REQUIREMENTS of the GIPS standards.

        ii. Is accurate.

        iii. Is consistent with the FIRM's records and policies and procedures.

    b. If model INVESTMENT MANAGEMENT FEES are used to calculate NET-OF-FEES returns, or model TOTAL POOLED FUND FEES are used to calculate POOLED FUND NET RETURNS, perform testing to determine that returns calculated using model fees are equal to or lower than those that would have been calculated using actual fees.

    c. Determine that the COMPOSITE or POOLED FUND BENCHMARK reflects the investment mandate, objective, or strategy of the COMPOSITE or POOLED FUND or, if the COMPOSITE or POOLED FUND has no BENCHMARK, that this is appropriate.

    d. If a custom BENCHMARK or combination of multiple BENCHMARKS is used, test the BENCHMARK data used by the FIRM to determine that the calculation methodology has been correctly applied and the data used are consistent with the BENCHMARK disclosure in the GIPS REPORT.

    e. Test BENCHMARK returns to determine that:

        i. The BENCHMARK returns are consistent with the returns published by the index provider.

        ii. Only TOTAL RETURN BENCHMARKS are used.

f. Determine that TOTAL FIRM ASSETS presented in the GIPS REPORT (or used in the calculation of COMPOSITE assets or POOLED FUND assets as a percentage of TOTAL FIRM ASSETS for periods ended prior to 1 January 2020) are consistent with TOTAL FIRM ASSETS tested in Step 5.

g. Review disclosures to determine that all REQUIRED disclosures are included and all disclosures are consistent with the FIRM's records and its policies and procedures.

h. If the GIPS REPORT includes total FIRM OVERLAY EXPOSURE, total FIRM ADVISORY-ONLY ASSETS, or total uncalled COMMITTED CAPITAL, determine that the disclosed amounts are accurate and consistent with supporting records.

i. If the GIPS REPORT includes SUPPLEMENTAL INFORMATION, determine that the SUPPLEMENTAL INFORMATION:

   i. Relates directly to the COMPOSITE or POOLED FUND.

   ii. Is not misleading, is clearly not false, and is not otherwise prohibited to be presented.

   iii. Is clearly labeled as SUPPLEMENTAL INFORMATION.

   iv. Does not contradict or conflict with the REQUIRED or RECOMMENDED information in the GIPS REPORT.

   v. Is not shown with greater prominence than the REQUIRED COMPOSITE or POOLED FUND information.

j. If the GIPS REPORT includes ported performance from a past firm or affiliation and the period(s) being verified includes performance from the past firm or affiliation, determine that:

   i. The REQUIREMENTS relating to investment decision makers, the decision-making process, and supporting records have been met.

   ii. If the performance is LINKED, there is no break in performance between the performance from the past firm or affiliation and the performance of the FIRM.

   iii. If there is a break in performance, the break is clearly shown.

   iv. The COMPOSITE performance from the past firm or affiliation includes all PORTFOLIOS that met the COMPOSITE DEFINITION at the past firm or affiliation.

   v. The POOLED FUND performance from the past firm or affiliation represents the performance of the POOLED FUND from the past firm or affiliation.

   vi. The GIPS REPORT includes the REQUIRED disclosures about the ported performance.

13. Providing GIPS REPORTS: Verifiers MUST perform sufficient procedures to determine that the FIRM has made every reasonable effort to provide the appropriate GIPS REPORT to PROSPECTIVE CLIENTS and LIMITED DISTRIBUTION POOLED FUND PROSPECTIVE INVESTORS.

14. Marketing Materials: Verifiers MUST gain an understanding of the FIRM's marketing practices, including whether the FIRM prepares GIPS ADVERTISEMENTS. Verifiers MUST select a sample

of marketing materials, including GIPS ADVERTISEMENTS, if applicable, and MUST perform the following procedures:

a. For each selection of marketing materials that includes a GIPS REPORT, verifiers MUST perform sufficient procedures to determine that:
   i. The GIPS REPORT includes all information REQUIRED by the GIPS standards.
   ii. The numerical information in the GIPS REPORT is accurate and consistent with the FIRM'S records and its policies and procedures.
   iii. The disclosures in the GIPS REPORT are consistent with the FIRM'S records and its policies and procedures.
b. For each GIPS ADVERTISEMENT, verifiers MUST perform sufficient procedures to determine that:
   i. The GIPS ADVERTISEMENT includes all information REQUIRED by the GIPS Advertising Guidelines.
   ii. The REQUIRED or RECOMMENDED numerical information is accurate and consistent with the FIRM'S records and its policies and procedures.
   iii. The disclosures are consistent with the FIRM'S records and its policies and procedures.
c. For each selection of marketing materials that is not a GIPS ADVERTISEMENT and does not include a GIPS REPORT, verifiers MUST perform sufficient procedures to determine that it does not include any improper references to the GIPS standards.

15. Error Correction: Verifiers MUST gain an understanding of errors in GIPS REPORTS that have occurred in, were identified in, or affect the period(s) being verified. If errors have occurred, verifiers MUST select errors for testing and perform sufficient procedures to determine that:
    a. The FIRM'S errors have been treated in accordance with the FIRM'S error correction policies and procedures.
    b. For MATERIAL ERRORS, the FIRM has 1) provided the corrected GIPS REPORT to current clients, current investors, and any former verifiers that received the GIPS REPORT that had the MATERIAL ERROR, as well as to the current verifier, and 2) made every reasonable effort to provide the corrected GIPS REPORT to current PROSPECTIVE CLIENTS and current PROSPECTIVE INVESTORS that received the GIPS REPORT that had the MATERIAL ERROR.
16. Notification to CFA Institute: Verifiers MUST perform sufficient procedures to determine that the FIRM has met the REQUIREMENT to notify CFA Institute of its claim of compliance with the GIPS standards by submitting the GIPS COMPLIANCE NOTIFICATION FORM.

Maintenance of Verifier Documentation

The verifier MUST maintain sufficient documentation of the following items for all VERIFICATION procedures performed that are necessary to support the VERIFICATION REPORT:

a. The nature, timing, and extent of all procedures performed, including planning procedures, sample size rationale, sample selections, and testing procedures applied;
b. The results of all procedures performed and the evidence obtained;
c. Significant findings or issues arising during the VERIFICATION, the conclusions reached thereon, and any significant professional judgments made in reaching those conclusions; and
d. Supporting evidence that the verifier has conducted all REQUIRED VERIFICATION procedures.

Representation Letter[1]

At the conclusion of the VERIFICATION engagement and prior to issuing the VERIFICATION REPORT, the verifier MUST obtain written representations signed by the FIRM's management who the verifier believes are responsible for and knowledgeable about the matters covered in the representations. The representation letter MUST include the following matters:

- The FIRM complies with the GIPS standards for all period(s) being verified;
- The FIRM's policies and procedures for establishing and maintaining compliance with the GIPS standards are properly described in the FIRM's GIPS standards policies and procedures;
- The FIRM's policies and procedures for complying with the GIPS standards have been designed in compliance with the GIPS standards and have been implemented on a FIRM-wide basis for all period(s) being verified;
- The FIRM is in compliance with the GIPS standards on a FIRM-wide basis;
- The FIRM's management bears all responsibility for maintaining compliance with the GIPS standards, including production and distribution of all GIPS REPORTS;
- The GIPS REPORTS are a fair and honest representation of the FIRM's investment performance;
- The FIRM has not knowingly presented performance or PERFORMANCE-RELATED INFORMATION that is false or misleading;
- To the best of the FIRM's knowledge and belief, there has been no:
  - fraud or alleged fraud involving management or employees who have significant roles in the FIRM's policies and procedures relating to compliance with the GIPS standards, or
  - fraud or alleged fraud involving others that could have a material effect on the FIRM's compliance with the GIPS standards.
- The FIRM has provided the verifier with all necessary documents to enable the verifier to perform the VERIFICATION, and no relevant documents have been withheld;
- The period(s) on which the verifier is reporting;

[1] Words in small capital letters are defined terms that can be found in the Glossary. These terms are not expected to be in small capital letters when included in a representation letter, VERIFICATION REPORT, or PERFORMANCE EXAMINATION REPORT.

- The FIRM complies with all applicable laws and regulations regarding the calculation and presentation of performance; and
- No events that would materially influence performance results or the outcome of the VERIFICATION have occurred up to the date of the representation letter.

The representation letter SHOULD also include any other relevant representations made to the verifier during the VERIFICATION.

Verification Report[2]

The VERIFICATION REPORT MUST opine that, for the period(s) for which the VERIFICATION has been performed, the FIRM's policies and procedures for complying with the GIPS standards related to COMPOSITE and POOLED FUND maintenance, as well as the calculation, presentation, and distribution of performance, have been, in all material respects:

- Designed in compliance with the GIPS standards; and
- Implemented on a FIRM-wide basis.

The following information is also REQUIRED to be included in the VERIFICATION REPORT:

- The report title, which MUST include the word "verification";
- The report date;
- The report addressee;
- The defined FIRM for which the VERIFICATION has been performed;
- The period(s) for which the VERIFICATION has been performed;
- The respective responsibilities of the FIRM's management and of the verifier, including a statement acknowledging the FIRM's responsibility for the claim of compliance;
- A statement to the effect that the VERIFICATION has been performed in accordance with the REQUIRED VERIFICATION procedures of the GIPS standards;
- A statement indicating that the VERIFICATION includes testing performed on a sample basis;
- Language indicating that the verifier is independent from the FIRM;
- A statement indicating that the VERIFICATION does not provide assurance on any specific performance report;
- A statement indicating that the VERIFICATION does not provide assurance on the operating effectiveness of the FIRM's controls or policies and procedures for complying with the GIPS standards;

[2] Words in small capital letters are defined terms that can be found in the Glossary. These terms are not expected to be in small capital letters when included in a representation letter, VERIFICATION REPORT, or PERFORMANCE EXAMINATION REPORT.

- A statement describing any other professional guidance that has been applied (e.g., AICPA, IAASB, ICAEW, or JICPA guidance);
- The following statement: "GIPS® is a registered trademark of CFA Institute. CFA Institute does not endorse or promote this organization, nor does it warrant the accuracy or quality of the content contained herein."; and
- The signature or official seal of the verifier.

In addition to the REQUIRED content, the VERIFICATION REPORT may also include other information, as appropriate.

After completing the VERIFICATION procedures, the verifier may conclude that the FIRM is not in compliance with the GIPS standards or that the FIRM'S records cannot support a VERIFICATION. In such situations, the verifier MUST inform the FIRM why a VERIFICATION REPORT could not be issued. A VERIFICATION REPORT MUST NOT be issued when the verifier knows that the FIRM is not in compliance with the GIPS standards or the records of the FIRM cannot support a VERIFICATION.

The FIRM MUST NOT state that it has been verified unless a VERIFICATION REPORT has been issued.

Recommendation Letter

After the VERIFICATION is complete, the verifier SHOULD issue a recommendation letter to the FIRM describing specific findings, recommendations, and other areas for improvement arising from the VERIFICATION.

PERFORMANCE EXAMINATION

Purpose and Scope of Performance Examination

In addition to VERIFICATION, a FIRM may choose to also have a PERFORMANCE EXAMINATION of a specific COMPOSITE or POOLED FUND. The detailed testing of any of the FIRM'S COMPOSITES or POOLED FUNDS and their associated GIPS REPORTS by an independent verifier is called a PERFORMANCE EXAMINATION.

A PERFORMANCE EXAMINATION may only be performed either concurrently with, or subsequent to the completion of, a VERIFICATION. The FIRM MUST be verified for the period(s) covered by the PERFORMANCE EXAMINATION REPORT. The VERIFICATION and the PERFORMANCE EXAMINATION need not be performed by the same verifier. The PERFORMANCE EXAMINATION MUST be performed by a qualified independent third party. Please see the Guidance Statement on Verifier Independence for additional guidance.

A PERFORMANCE EXAMINATION is not REQUIRED for a FIRM to be verified and is neither RECOMMENDED nor REQUIRED under the GIPS standards. However, a FIRM may be asked or may choose to obtain a PERFORMANCE EXAMINATION of one or more of the FIRM'S COMPOSITES or POOLED FUNDS.

A PERFORMANCE EXAMINATION tests, for a specific COMPOSITE:

a. Whether the FIRM has constructed the COMPOSITE and calculated the COMPOSITE performance in compliance with the GIPS standards, and
b. Whether the FIRM has prepared and presented the GIPS COMPOSITE REPORT in compliance with the GIPS standards.

A PERFORMANCE EXAMINATION tests, for a specific POOLED FUND:

a. Whether the FIRM has calculated the POOLED FUND performance in compliance with the GIPS standards, and
b. Whether the FIRM has prepared and presented the GIPS POOLED FUND REPORT in compliance with the GIPS standards.

ASSET OWNERS may also choose to have a PERFORMANCE EXAMINATION for any TOTAL FUND or COMPOSITE. The 2020 edition of the GIPS Standards for Verifiers does not include PERFORMANCE EXAMINATION guidance specific to ASSET OWNERS. When considering this guidance for conducting a PERFORMANCE EXAMINATION for an ASSET OWNER, verifiers MUST interpret references to FIRMS as also referring to ASSET OWNERS, and they MUST interpret references to COMPOSITES as also referring to TOTAL FUNDS and additional COMPOSITES. Verifiers that conduct PERFORMANCE EXAMINATIONS for ASSET OWNERS MUST follow the REQUIRED PERFORMANCE EXAMINATION procedures to the extent possible, and they MUST tailor these procedures to fit the unique facts and circumstances of the ASSET OWNER. Verifiers MUST document their rationale for their testing approach, including why any REQUIRED PERFORMANCE EXAMINATION procedure was modified or not appropriate.

Verifier Qualification Requirements

The PERFORMANCE EXAMINATION MUST be performed by a qualified independent third party:

- Verifiers MUST have appropriate professional abilities and experience, as well as a practical level of expertise regarding audit methodology and investment management practices, including investment accounting, performance calculation methodologies, and business processes.
- Verifiers MUST be knowledgeable about the GIPS standards and MUST understand all the REQUIREMENTS and RECOMMENDATIONS of the GIPS standards, including all applicable Guidance Statements, interpretations, and Questions & Answers (Q&As) published by CFA Institute and the GIPS standards governing bodies.
- Verifiers MUST also be knowledgeable about applicable laws and regulations regarding the calculation and presentation of performance.

The verifier MUST be independent from the FIRM. Please see the Guidance Statement on Verifier Independence for additional guidance.

Verifiers are auditing, consulting, and other firms that have a high degree of knowledge regarding the investment management industry. Verifiers MUST follow any applicable professional guidance and standards of practice within their industry when performing a PERFORMANCE EXAMINATION.

Agreeing on the Terms of the Engagement

Prior to commencing the engagement, the verifier MUST agree on the terms of the PERFORMANCE EXAMINATION with the FIRM. The agreed terms MUST be specified in an engagement letter or other suitable form of written agreement and MUST include the following:

a. The objective and scope of the engagement, including the period(s) being examined;

b. The verifier's responsibilities;

c. The FIRM's responsibilities;

d. A statement about the inherent limitations of a PERFORMANCE EXAMINATION;

e. A statement that the GIPS standards are the evaluation criteria for the engagement; and

f. A statement that the FIRM agrees to provide the verifier with a representation letter at the conclusion of the PERFORMANCE EXAMINATION.

The engagement letter SHOULD also include any other terms and conditions relevant to the PERFORMANCE EXAMINATION.

Required Performance Examination Procedures

A PERFORMANCE EXAMINATION MUST be conducted in accordance with the REQUIRED PERFORMANCE EXAMINATION procedures of the GIPS standards. The following are the minimum procedures verifiers MUST perform when conducting a PERFORMANCE EXAMINATION. Verifiers MUST complete the PERFORMANCE EXAMINATION in accordance with these procedures prior to issuing a PERFORMANCE EXAMINATION REPORT to the FIRM.

Planning Procedures

The verifier MUST consider the following presumptions:

- Information obtained from independent third parties provides greater assurance than the same information obtained from the FIRM;
- Information obtained from the verifier's direct personal knowledge (such as through tangible documentation, observation, computation, operating tests, or inspection) is more persuasive than information obtained indirectly; and
- Information obtained from a FIRM with an effective control environment is more reliable than information obtained from a FIRM without an effective control environment.

The verifier MUST consider the following matters when designing test procedures:

- The nature and materiality of the information to be tested;
- The control environment (including the extent to which automated and manual processes are used);
- The likelihood of misstatements;
- Knowledge obtained during current and previous engagements;
- The extent to which the information is affected by judgment; and
- Inadequacies in the underlying data.

When conducting a PERFORMANCE EXAMINATION, the verifier MUST accumulate sufficient evidence and perform sufficient procedures such that the risk of not detecting errors during the PERFORMANCE EXAMINATION is mitigated to an acceptably low level.

Testing by inquiry on its own is insufficient to satisfy the REQUIRED PERFORMANCE EXAMINATION procedures when other testing procedures could reasonably be performed (e.g., inspection, observation, or recalculation). Verifiers MUST review sufficient and appropriate supporting documentation when conducting PERFORMANCE EXAMINATION procedures.

A verifier may choose to rely on the audit and/or internal control work of a qualified and reputable independent third party. In addition, a verifier may choose to rely on other audit and/or internal control work it has provided to the FIRM. A verifier may also accept the VERIFICATION work of another verifier as part of the basis for the verifier's PERFORMANCE EXAMINATION REPORT. If the verifier plans to rely on work performed by another party, then the work—including scope, period(s) covered, results of procedures performed, and the other party's qualifications, competency, objectivity, and reputation—MUST be assessed by the verifier when determining whether to place any reliance on such work. Reliance considerations and conclusions MUST be documented by the verifier. The verifier MUST use professional skepticism when deciding whether to place reliance on work performed by another party.

Sample Selection: Composites

Verifiers MUST subject the entire COMPOSITE to testing when conducting PERFORMANCE EXAMINATION procedures. Verifiers may use a sampling methodology when performing such testing procedures. The verifier MUST determine not only the appropriate sample size but also whether the sample selected is reasonable considering the FIRM's specific circumstances. The verifier MUST select samples from the entire period(s) being examined.

Verifiers MUST consider the following criteria when selecting samples:

- Number of PORTFOLIOS in the COMPOSITE;
- COMPOSITE DEFINITION;
- Individual PORTFOLIO assets relative to total COMPOSITE assets;
- Internal control environment at the FIRM;
- Number of years being examined;
- Systems used in the construction and maintenance of COMPOSITES;
- Methodology and systems used for calculating and reporting performance; and
- The use of external service providers.

This list is not all-inclusive and contains only the minimum criteria that MUST be considered in the selection and evaluation of a sample. For example, one potentially useful approach for a COMPOSITE PERFORMANCE EXAMINATION would be to include in the sample a PORTFOLIO that has the largest effect on COMPOSITE performance because of its size. Missing or incomplete documents, or the presence of errors, would warrant selecting a larger sample or applying additional PERFORMANCE EXAMINATION procedures.

Sample Selection: Pooled Funds

Verifiers MUST subject the entire POOLED FUND track record covered by the PERFORMANCE EXAMINATION to testing when conducting PERFORMANCE EXAMINATION procedures. Verifiers may use a sampling methodology when performing such testing procedures. The verifier MUST determine not only the appropriate sample size but also whether the sample selected is reasonable considering the FIRM's specific circumstances. The verifier MUST select samples from the entire period(s) being examined.

Verifiers MUST consider the following criteria when selecting samples:

- POOLED FUND strategy and legal structure;
- Internal control environment at the FIRM;
- Number of years being examined;
- Methodology and systems used for calculating and reporting performance; and
- The use of external service providers.

This list is not all-inclusive and contains only the minimum criteria that MUST be considered in the selection and evaluation of a sample. Missing or incomplete documents, or the presence of errors, would warrant selecting a larger sample or applying additional PERFORMANCE EXAMINATION procedures.

Testing Procedures

1. Recordkeeping: While conducting the REQUIRED testing procedures, verifiers MUST determine whether:
    a. The FIRM has captured and maintained the data and information necessary to support all items included in the GIPS REPORT.
    b. The data and information are available within a reasonable time frame.

    Detailed examples of data and information that could be examined are provided in the Guidance Statement on Recordkeeping Requirements.
2. Policies and Procedures: Verifiers MUST obtain the FIRM's policies and procedures used in establishing and maintaining compliance with the GIPS standards that are relevant to the COMPOSITE or POOLED FUND being examined. Verifiers MUST understand the FIRM's policies and procedures for establishing and maintaining compliance with all the applicable REQUIREMENTS and adopted RECOMMENDATIONS of the GIPS standards that are relevant to the COMPOSITE or POOLED FUND being examined. Verifiers MUST perform sufficient procedures to determine that, with respect to the COMPOSITE or POOLED FUND being examined:
    a. The FIRM's policies and procedures are consistent with the GIPS standards;
    b. The FIRM's policies and procedures are complete, clear, unambiguous, and adequately documented; and

 |

c. The FIRM's policies and procedures are suitably designed to enable the FIRM to:
    i. Construct the COMPOSITE, calculate COMPOSITE performance, and prepare and present the GIPS COMPOSITE REPORT in compliance with the GIPS standards; or
    ii. Calculate POOLED FUND performance and prepare and present the GIPS POOLED FUND REPORT in compliance with the GIPS standards.

3. FIRM Definition: Verifiers MUST gain an understanding of the FIRM, including the corporate structure of the FIRM and how it operates.
4. Assignment of PORTFOLIOS to COMPOSITES (COMPOSITES only): The verifier MUST obtain a list of all open (both new and existing) and terminated PORTFOLIOS for the COMPOSITE for the period(s) under examination, including each PORTFOLIO's returns and values for all periods, and perform sufficient procedures to determine, for the COMPOSITE being examined, that:
    a. The FIRM has defined and maintained the COMPOSITE in compliance with the GIPS standards.
    b. The FIRM's policies and procedures for creating and maintaining the COMPOSITE have been consistently applied.
    c. PORTFOLIOS included in the COMPOSITE are properly classified as discretionary, as indicated by the PORTFOLIO's investment management agreement, investment guidelines, and other appropriate documentation.
    d. The investment mandate, objective, or strategy of PORTFOLIOS included in the COMPOSITE, as indicated by the PORTFOLIO's investment management agreement, investment guidelines, PORTFOLIO holdings, and other appropriate documentation, is consistent with the COMPOSITE DEFINITION.
    e. The timing of inclusion of new PORTFOLIOS in the COMPOSITE is in accordance with the FIRM's new PORTFOLIO policies and procedures.
    f. The timing of exclusion of terminated PORTFOLIOS from the COMPOSITE is in accordance with the FIRM's terminated PORTFOLIO policies and procedures.
    g. Movements of PORTFOLIOS into and out of the COMPOSITE are appropriate, consistent either with documented changes to a PORTFOLIO's investment mandate, objective, or strategy or with the redefinition of the COMPOSITE, and in accordance with the FIRM's policies and procedures for moved PORTFOLIOS.
    h. If the COMPOSITE has a COMPOSITE minimum asset level, PORTFOLIOS are included in and excluded from the COMPOSITE in accordance with the FIRM's minimum asset level policies and procedures.
    i. If the COMPOSITE has a SIGNIFICANT CASH FLOW policy, PORTFOLIOS are included in and excluded from the COMPOSITE in accordance with the FIRM'S SIGNIFICANT CASH FLOW policies and procedures.
    j. If the COMPOSITE excludes non-fee-paying PORTFOLIOS, non-fee-paying PORTFOLIOS are excluded from the COMPOSITE in accordance with the FIRM's non-fee-paying PORTFOLIO policies and procedures.

5. Outlier Returns (COMPOSITES only): Verifiers MUST perform sufficient procedures to determine that outlier returns within the COMPOSITE being examined do not indicate PORTFOLIO return or COMPOSITE assignment errors. Verifiers MUST:
   a. Review PORTFOLIO returns within the COMPOSITE being examined, to identify PORTFOLIOS with returns that significantly deviate from the returns of other PORTFOLIOS within the COMPOSITE.
   b. Select all PORTFOLIOS with outlier returns and for each PORTFOLIO determine that:
      i. There are no input data or PORTFOLIO return calculation errors relating to the outlier returns.
      ii. The PORTFOLIO is properly included in the COMPOSITE being examined.
6. EXTERNAL CASH FLOWS: Verifiers MUST determine that EXTERNAL CASH FLOWS for PORTFOLIOS in the COMPOSITE being examined or for the POOLED FUND being examined are:
   - Properly recorded in PORTFOLIOS;
   - Recorded at the correct amounts;
   - Properly identified as a LARGE CASH FLOW (as defined by the FIRM's policies and procedures); and
   - Recorded on a timely basis in accordance with the FIRM's policies and procedures.

   Verifiers MUST perform sufficient procedures to determine that:
   a. EXTERNAL CASH FLOWS reflect appropriate supporting documentation, such as custody statements, client subscription and redemption notifications, or internal records;
   b. EXTERNAL CASH FLOWS reflect proper valuation and timely recording; and
   c. The recording of EXTERNAL CASH FLOWS is appropriate and in accordance with the FIRM's policies and procedures.
7. Income and Expenses: Verifiers MUST determine that income and expenses for PORTFOLIOS in the COMPOSITE being examined or for the POOLED FUND being examined are:
   - Properly recorded in PORTFOLIOS;
   - Recorded at the correct amounts; and
   - Recorded on a timely basis.

   Verifiers MUST perform sufficient procedures to determine that the treatment of the following items is consistent with the FIRM's policies and procedures:
   a. Classification of PORTFOLIO flows (e.g., receipts, disbursements, dividends, interest, fees, expenses, and taxes);
   b. Accounting treatment of dividend and interest income;
   c. Accounting treatment of taxes, tax reclaims, and tax accruals;
   d. Accounting treatment of TRANSACTION COSTS;
   e. Accounting treatment of fees and expenses; and
   f. Accounting treatment of and valuation methodologies for investments.

8. PORTFOLIO Valuation: Verifiers MUST determine that investments, including derivatives, for PORTFOLIOS in the COMPOSITE being examined or for the POOLED FUND being examined are:
   - Valued correctly; and
   - Valued on the correct dates.

   Verifiers MUST perform sufficient procedures to determine that:
   a. PORTFOLIO holdings are complete and accurate, as well as consistent with appropriate documentation such as custody statements and reconciliations;
   b. Investment valuations are in accordance with the FIRM's valuation policies and procedures, as well as the GIPS standards valuation REQUIREMENTS;
   c. PORTFOLIOS are valued on the date of all LARGE CASH FLOWS in accordance with the FIRM's policies and procedures;
   d. Foreign currency exchange rates are in accordance with the FIRM's valuation policies; and
   e. The method(s) used for PORTFOLIO valuation are consistently applied.
9. Performance Based on Actual Assets: For the COMPOSITE or POOLED FUND being examined, verifiers MUST perform sufficient procedures to determine that PORTFOLIO holdings, income, and cash flows are supported by appropriate documents from independent third parties, if applicable. Examples of appropriate documents include custodian, fund accounting, and broker statements, as well as client subscription and redemption notifications.
10. Performance Measurement: Verifiers MUST perform sufficient procedures to determine that the FIRM has calculated performance for the COMPOSITE or POOLED FUND being examined in accordance with the REQUIREMENTS of the GIPS standards and the FIRM's policies and procedures. Verifiers MUST, for a sample of PORTFOLIO and COMPOSITE returns, recalculate returns to determine that:
    a. An acceptable return formula as REQUIRED by the GIPS standards is used.
    b. The FIRM's calculations, including the treatment of any fees and expenses, are in accordance with the FIRM's policies and procedures.
11. GIPS REPORTS: Verifiers MUST perform sufficient procedures on the GIPS REPORT for the COMPOSITE being examined or for the POOLED FUND being examined to determine that the GIPS REPORT includes all the numerical information and disclosures REQUIRED by the GIPS standards and that any other information included beyond the REQUIRED information is appropriate.

    Verifiers MUST perform the following procedures:
    a. Test COMPOSITE, or POOLED FUND, and BENCHMARK calculations to determine that all presented numerical information, except SUPPLEMENTAL INFORMATION:
       i. Adheres to the REQUIREMENTS of the GIPS standards.
       ii. Is accurate.
       iii. Is consistent with the FIRM's records and its policies and procedures.

b. If model INVESTMENT MANAGEMENT FEES are used to calculate NET-OF-FEES returns, or model TOTAL POOLED FUND FEES are used to calculate POOLED FUND NET RETURNS, perform testing to determine that returns calculated using model fees are equal to or lower than those that would have been calculated using actual fees.

c. Determine that the COMPOSITE or POOLED FUND BENCHMARK reflects the investment mandate, objective, or strategy of the COMPOSITE or POOLED FUND or, if the COMPOSITE or POOLED FUND has no BENCHMARK, that this is appropriate.

d. If a custom BENCHMARK or combination of multiple BENCHMARKS is used, test the BENCHMARK data used by the FIRM to determine that the calculation methodology has been correctly applied and the data used are consistent with the BENCHMARK disclosure in the GIPS REPORT.

e. Test BENCHMARK returns to determine that:

   i. The BENCHMARK returns are consistent with the returns published by the index provider.

   ii. Only TOTAL RETURN BENCHMARKS are used.

f. Review disclosures to determine that all REQUIRED disclosures are included and all disclosures are consistent with the FIRM's records and policies and procedures.

g. If the GIPS REPORT includes total FIRM OVERLAY EXPOSURE, total FIRM ADVISORY-ONLY ASSETS, or total uncalled COMMITTED CAPITAL, determine that the disclosed amounts are accurate and consistent with the FIRM's supporting records.

h. If the GIPS REPORT includes SUPPLEMENTAL INFORMATION, determine that the SUPPLEMENTAL INFORMATION:

   i. Relates directly to the COMPOSITE or POOLED FUND.

   ii. Is not misleading, is clearly not false, and is not otherwise prohibited to be presented.

   iii. Is clearly labeled as SUPPLEMENTAL INFORMATION.

   iv. Does not contradict or conflict with the REQUIRED or RECOMMENDED information in the GIPS REPORT.

   v. Is not shown with greater prominence than the REQUIRED COMPOSITE or POOLED FUND information.

   The FIRM and verifier MUST decide if the SUPPLEMENTAL INFORMATION is subject to the PERFORMANCE EXAMINATION and, if so, the verifier MUST also determine that the SUPPLEMENTAL INFORMATION is accurate and consistent with the FIRM's records and policies and procedures.

i. If the GIPS REPORT includes ported performance from a past firm or affiliation and the period(s) being examined includes performance from the past firm or affiliation, determine that:

   i. The REQUIREMENTS relating to investment decision makers, the decision-making process, and supporting records have been met.

   ii. If the performance is LINKED, there is no break in performance between the performance from the past firm or affiliation and the performance of the FIRM.
   iii. If there is a break in performance, the break is clearly shown.
   iv. The COMPOSITE performance from the past firm or affiliation includes all PORTFOLIOS that met the COMPOSITE DEFINITION at the past firm or affiliation.
   v. The POOLED FUND performance from the past firm or affiliation represents the performance of the POOLED FUND from the past firm or affiliation.
   vi. The GIPS REPORT includes the REQUIRED disclosures about the ported performance.

j. Error correction: Verifiers MUST gain an understanding of errors in the GIPS REPORT that have occurred in, were identified in, or affect the period(s) being examined. If errors have occurred, verifiers MUST select errors for testing and perform sufficient procedures to determine that:
   i. The FIRM'S errors have been treated in accordance with the FIRM'S error correction policies and procedures.
   ii. For MATERIAL ERRORS, the FIRM has 1) provided the corrected GIPS REPORT to all current clients, current investors, and any former verifiers that received the GIPS REPORT that had the MATERIAL ERROR, as well as to the current verifier, and 2) made every reasonable effort to provide the corrected GIPS REPORT to current PROSPECTIVE CLIENTS and current PROSPECTIVE INVESTORS that received the GIPS REPORT that had the MATERIAL ERROR.

Maintenance of Verifier Documentation

The verifier MUST maintain sufficient documentation of the following items for all PERFORMANCE EXAMINATION procedures performed that are necessary to support the PERFORMANCE EXAMINATION REPORT:

a. The nature, timing, and extent of all procedures performed, including planning procedures, sample size rationale, sample selections, and testing procedures applied;
b. The results of all procedures performed and the evidence obtained;
c. Significant findings or issues arising during the PERFORMANCE EXAMINATION, the conclusions reached thereon, and any significant professional judgments made in reaching those conclusions; and
d. Supporting evidence that the verifier has conducted all REQUIRED PERFORMANCE EXAMINATION procedures.

Representation Letter[3]

At the conclusion of the PERFORMANCE EXAMINATION engagement and prior to issuing the PERFORMANCE EXAMINATION REPORT, the verifier conducting the PERFORMANCE EXAMINATION MUST obtain written representations signed by the FIRM's management who the verifier believes are responsible for and knowledgeable about the matters covered in the representations. The representation letter MUST include the following matters:

- The FIRM complies with the GIPS standards for all period(s) being examined;
- The FIRM's policies and procedures for establishing and maintaining compliance with the GIPS standards are properly described in the FIRM's GIPS standards policies and procedures;
- The FIRM's policies and procedures for complying with the GIPS standards have been designed in compliance with the GIPS standards and have been implemented on a FIRM-wide basis for all period(s) being examined;
- The FIRM is in compliance with the GIPS standards on a FIRM-wide basis;
- The FIRM has constructed the COMPOSITE and calculated the COMPOSITE's performance in compliance with the GIPS standards, or the FIRM has calculated the POOLED FUND's performance in compliance with the GIPS standards;
- The FIRM has prepared and presented the GIPS COMPOSITE REPORT or GIPS POOLED FUND REPORT in compliance with the GIPS standards;
- The FIRM's management bears all responsibility for maintaining compliance with the GIPS standards, including production and distribution of the GIPS COMPOSITE REPORT or GIPS POOLED FUND REPORT;
- The GIPS COMPOSITE REPORT or GIPS POOLED FUND REPORT is a fair and accurate representation of the FIRM's investment performance;
- The FIRM has not knowingly presented performance or PERFORMANCE-RELATED INFORMATION for the COMPOSITE being examined or for the POOLED FUND being examined that is false or misleading;
- To the best of the FIRM's knowledge and belief, there has been no:
    - fraud or alleged fraud involving management or employees who have significant roles in the FIRM's policies and procedures relating to compliance with the GIPS standards, or
    - fraud or alleged fraud involving others that could have a material effect on the FIRM's compliance with the GIPS standards;
- The FIRM has provided the verifier with all necessary documents to enable the verifier to perform the PERFORMANCE EXAMINATION, and no relevant documents have been withheld;
- The period(s) on which the verifier is reporting;

[3] Words in small capital letters are defined terms that can be found in the Glossary. These terms are not expected to be in small capital letters when included in a representation letter, VERIFICATION REPORT, or PERFORMANCE EXAMINATION REPORT.

- The FIRM complies with all applicable laws and regulations regarding the calculation and presentation of performance for the COMPOSITE being examined or for the POOLED FUND being examined; and
- No events that would materially influence performance results or the outcome of the PERFORMANCE EXAMINATION have occurred up to the date of the representation letter.

The representation letter SHOULD also include any other relevant representations made to the verifier during the PERFORMANCE EXAMINATION.

Performance Examination Report[4]

If PERFORMANCE EXAMINATIONS are performed on multiple COMPOSITES or POOLED FUNDS and their associated GIPS REPORTS, the verifier may issue a single PERFORMANCE EXAMINATION REPORT covering the COMPOSITES or POOLED FUNDS and their associated GIPS REPORTS that have been examined. The PERFORMANCE EXAMINATION REPORT can be prepared either as part of a VERIFICATION REPORT (combined report) or as a separate report attached to the VERIFICATION REPORT. The GIPS REPORT for any COMPOSITE or POOLED FUND that has been examined MUST be included in or attached to the PERFORMANCE EXAMINATION REPORT.

1) In order for a PERFORMANCE EXAMINATION REPORT to be issued, the verifier MUST ensure that the FIRM has received a VERIFICATION REPORT(S) covering the period(s) being examined.
2) A PERFORMANCE EXAMINATION REPORT MUST NOT cover period(s) beyond those period(s) covered by the VERIFICATION REPORT(S). A PERFORMANCE EXAMINATION REPORT MUST NOT be issued prior to the VERIFICATION REPORT.
3) Because a VERIFICATION is REQUIRED in order to receive a PERFORMANCE EXAMINATION, the PERFORMANCE EXAMINATION REPORT MUST include the period(s) for which the FIRM has been verified.
4) For a COMPOSITE, the PERFORMANCE EXAMINATION REPORT MUST opine that, for the period(s) for which the PERFORMANCE EXAMINATION has been performed, the FIRM has, in all material respects:
    - Constructed the COMPOSITE and calculated the COMPOSITE performance in compliance with the GIPS standards, and
    - Prepared and presented the GIPS COMPOSITE REPORT in compliance with the GIPS standards.

    For a POOLED FUND, the PERFORMANCE EXAMINATION REPORT MUST opine that, for the period(s) for which the PERFORMANCE EXAMINATION has been performed, the FIRM has, in all material respects:

[4] Words in small capital letters are defined terms that can be found in the Glossary. These terms are not expected to be in small capital letters when included in a representation letter, VERIFICATION REPORT, or PERFORMANCE EXAMINATION REPORT.

- Calculated the POOLED FUND performance in compliance with the GIPS standards, and
- Prepared and presented the GIPS POOLED FUND REPORT in compliance with the GIPS standards.

The following information is also REQUIRED to be included in the PERFORMANCE EXAMINATION REPORT:

- The report title, which MUST include the words "performance examination";
- The report date;
- The report addressee;
- The defined FIRM for which the VERIFICATION has been performed;
- The period(s) for which the VERIFICATION has been performed;
- The respective responsibilities of the FIRM'S management and of the verifier, including a statement acknowledging the FIRM'S responsibility for the claim of compliance and for the GIPS COMPOSITE REPORT or GIPS POOLED FUND REPORT;
- The period(s) for which the PERFORMANCE EXAMINATION has been performed;
- For COMPOSITES:
  - The name of the COMPOSITE that has been examined;
  - A statement indicating that the PERFORMANCE EXAMINATION of the specified COMPOSITE and its associated GIPS COMPOSITE REPORT has been performed in accordance with the REQUIRED PERFORMANCE EXAMINATION procedures of the GIPS standards;
- For POOLED FUNDS:
  - The name of the POOLED FUND that has been examined;
  - A statement indicating that the PERFORMANCE EXAMINATION of the specified POOLED FUND and its associated GIPS POOLED FUND REPORT has been performed in accordance with the REQUIRED PERFORMANCE EXAMINATION procedures of the GIPS standards;
- A statement indicating that the PERFORMANCE EXAMINATION includes testing performed on a sample basis;
- Language indicating that the verifier is independent from the FIRM;
- A statement indicating that the PERFORMANCE EXAMINATION does not provide assurance on any other specific COMPOSITE or POOLED FUND performance report;
- A statement indicating whether or not the PERFORMANCE EXAMINATION covers SUPPLEMENTAL INFORMATION included in the GIPS COMPOSITE REPORT or GIPS POOLED FUND REPORT, if applicable;
- A statement describing any other professional guidance that has been applied (e.g., AICPA, IAASB, ICAEW, or JICPA guidance);

- The following statement: "GIPS® is a registered trademark of CFA Institute. CFA Institute does not endorse or promote this organization, nor does it warrant the accuracy or quality of the content contained herein."; and
- The signature or official seal of the verifier.

In addition to the REQUIRED content, the PERFORMANCE EXAMINATION REPORT may also include other information, as appropriate.

5) After completing the PERFORMANCE EXAMINATION procedures, the verifier may conclude that the GIPS REPORT does not comply with the GIPS standards or that the FIRM's records cannot support the PERFORMANCE EXAMINATION. In such situations, the verifier and the FIRM MUST consider the effect of the verifier's inability to issue the PERFORMANCE EXAMINATION REPORT on the FIRM's claim of compliance with the GIPS standards. A PERFORMANCE EXAMINATION REPORT MUST NOT be issued when the verifier knows that the FIRM is not in compliance with the GIPS standards, the GIPS REPORT does not comply with the GIPS standards, or the records of the FIRM cannot support the examination of the specific COMPOSITE or POOLED FUND and its associated GIPS REPORT. When a PERFORMANCE EXAMINATION REPORT cannot be issued, the verifier MUST inform the FIRM why a PERFORMANCE EXAMINATION REPORT cannot be issued.
6) The FIRM MUST NOT state that a COMPOSITE or POOLED FUND has been examined unless a PERFORMANCE EXAMINATION REPORT has been issued.

Recommendation Letter

After the PERFORMANCE EXAMINATION is complete, the verifier SHOULD issue a recommendation letter to the FIRM describing specific findings, recommendations, and other areas for improvement arising from the PERFORMANCE EXAMINATION.

EFFECTIVE DATE

GIPS COMPOSITE REPORTS, GIPS POOLED FUND REPORTS, and GIPS ASSET OWNER REPORTS that include performance results for periods ending on or after 31 December 2020 MUST be prepared in accordance with the 2020 edition of the GIPS standards. FIRMS and ASSET OWNERS may early adopt the 2020 edition of the GIPS standards.

Verifiers MUST conduct their VERIFICATION and PERFORMANCE EXAMINATION engagements in accordance with the 2020 edition of the GIPS Standards for Verifiers for periods for which the FIRM or ASSET OWNER claims compliance following the 2020 edition of the GIPS standards. Verifiers are RECOMMENDED to conduct their VERIFICATION and PERFORMANCE EXAMINATION engagements in accordance with the 2020 edition of the GIPS Standards for Verifiers for all periods for which they are conducting the engagement.

GLOSSARY

ADMINISTRATIVE FEE — All fees other than TRANSACTION COSTS and the INVESTMENT MANAGEMENT FEE. ADMINISTRATIVE FEES may include CUSTODY FEES, accounting fees, auditing fees, consulting fees, legal fees, performance measurement fees, and other related fees.

ADVISORY-ONLY ASSETS — Assets for which the FIRM provides investment recommendations but has no control over implementation of investment decisions and no trading authority.

ASSET OWNER — An entity that manages investments, directly and/or through the use of EXTERNAL MANAGERS, on behalf of participants, beneficiaries, or the organization itself. These entities include, but are not limited to, public and private pension funds, endowments, foundations, family offices, provident funds, insurers and reinsurers, sovereign wealth funds, and fiduciaries. ASSET OWNERS MUST have discretion over TOTAL ASSET OWNER ASSETS, either by managing assets directly or by having the discretion to hire and fire EXTERNAL MANAGERS.

BENCHMARK — A point of reference against which the COMPOSITE'S, POOLED FUND'S, or TOTAL FUND'S returns or risk are compared.

BROAD DISTRIBUTION POOLED FUND — A POOLED FUND that is regulated under a framework that would permit the general public to purchase or hold the POOLED FUND'S shares and is not exclusively offered in one-on-one presentations.

CARRIED INTEREST — The profits that the GENERAL PARTNER is allocated from the profits on the investments made by the investment vehicle. Also known as "carry" or "promote."

CLOSED-END — A POOLED FUND that is not open for subscriptions and/or redemptions.

COMMITTED CAPITAL — Pledges of capital to an investment vehicle by investors (LIMITED PARTNERS and the GENERAL PARTNER), the FIRM, or the ASSET OWNER. COMMITTED CAPITAL is typically drawn down over a period of time. Also known as "commitments."

COMPOSITE — An aggregation of one or more PORTFOLIOS or TOTAL FUNDS that are managed according to a similar investment mandate, objective, or strategy.

(continued)

COMPOSITE DEFINITION

Detailed criteria that determine the assignment of PORTFOLIOS to COMPOSITES. Criteria may include, but are not limited to, investment mandate, style or strategy, asset class, the use of derivatives, leverage and/or hedging, targeted risk metrics, investment constraints or restrictions, and/or PORTFOLIO type (e.g., SEGREGATED ACCOUNT or POOLED FUND, taxable versus tax exempt).

COMPOSITE DESCRIPTION

General information regarding the investment mandate, objective, or strategy of the COMPOSITE. The COMPOSITE DESCRIPTION may be more abbreviated than the COMPOSITE DEFINITION but MUST include all key features of the COMPOSITE and MUST include enough information to allow a PROSPECTIVE CLIENT to understand the key characteristics of the COMPOSITE'S investment mandate, objective, or strategy, including:

- The material risks of the COMPOSITE'S strategy.
- How leverage, derivatives, and short positions may be used, if they are a material part of the strategy.
- If ILLIQUID INVESTMENTS are a material part of the strategy.

CUSTODY FEE

The fee payable to the custodian for the safekeeping of PORTFOLIO assets. CUSTODY FEES are considered to be ADMINISTRATIVE FEES and typically contain an asset-based portion and a transaction-based portion. The CUSTODY FEE may also include charges for additional services, including accounting, securities lending, and/or performance measurement. Custodial fees that are charged per transaction SHOULD be included in the CUSTODY FEE and not included as part of TRANSACTION COSTS.

EXTERNAL CASH FLOW

Capital (cash or investments) that enters or exits a PORTFOLIO. Dividend and interest income payments are not considered EXTERNAL CASH FLOWS.

EXTERNAL MANAGER

A third-party investment manager hired by an ASSET OWNER to manage some or all of the TOTAL ASSET OWNER ASSETS.

FIRM

The entity defined for compliance with the GIPS standards.

FIXED LIFE

Having a predetermined, finite investment time horizon.

GENERAL PARTNER

Typically, the manager of a LIMITED PARTNERSHIP in which the LIMITED PARTNERS are the other investors. The GENERAL PARTNER earns an INVESTMENT MANAGEMENT FEE that may include a percentage of the LIMITED PARTNERSHIP'S profits. (See "CARRIED INTEREST.")

GIPS ADVERTISEMENT	An advertisement by a GIPS-compliant FIRM or ASSET OWNER that adheres to the REQUIREMENTS of the GIPS Advertising Guidelines.
GIPS ASSET OWNER REPORT	An ASSET OWNER's presentation for a TOTAL FUND or COMPOSITE that contains all the information REQUIRED by the GIPS standards and may also include RECOMMENDED information or SUPPLEMENTAL INFORMATION.
GIPS COMPLIANCE NOTIFICATION FORM	The form REQUIRED to be filed with CFA Institute to notify CFA Institute that the FIRM or ASSET OWNER claims compliance with the GIPS standards.
GIPS COMPOSITE REPORT	A presentation for a COMPOSITE that contains all the information REQUIRED by the GIPS standards and may also include RECOMMENDED information or SUPPLEMENTAL INFORMATION.
GIPS POOLED FUND REPORT	A presentation for a POOLED FUND that contains all the information REQUIRED by the GIPS standards and may also include RECOMMENDED information or SUPPLEMENTAL INFORMATION.
GIPS REPORT	Either a GIPS COMPOSITE REPORT or a GIPS POOLED FUND REPORT.
GROSS-OF-FEES	For FIRMS, the return on investments reduced by any TRANSACTION COSTS. For ASSET OWNERS, the return on investments reduced by TRANSACTION COSTS and all fees and expenses for externally managed POOLED FUNDS.
ILLIQUID INVESTMENTS	Investments that may be difficult to sell without a price reduction or that cannot be sold quickly because of a lack of market or ready/willing investors.
INVESTMENT MANAGEMENT COSTS	All costs for both internally and externally managed assets. In addition to costs for PORTFOLIO management, they may also involve overhead and other related costs and fees, including data valuation fees, investment research services, CUSTODY FEES, pro rata share of overhead (such as building and utilities), allocation of non-investment-department expenses (such as human resources, communications, and technology), and performance measurement and compliance services.

(continued)

INVESTMENT MANAGEMENT FEE

For FIRMS, a fee payable to the FIRM for management of a PORTFOLIO. INVESTMENT MANAGEMENT FEES are typically asset based (percentage of assets), performance based (see "PERFORMANCE-BASED FEE"), or a combination of the two but may take different forms as well. INVESTMENT MANAGEMENT FEES also include CARRIED INTEREST.

For ASSET OWNERS, a fee payable to EXTERNAL MANAGERS for externally managed assets. INVESTMENT MANAGEMENT FEES are typically asset based (percentage of assets), performance based (see "PERFORMANCE-BASED FEE"), or a combination of the two but may take different forms as well. INVESTMENT MANAGEMENT FEES also include CARRIED INTEREST.

LARGE CASH FLOW

The level at which the FIRM or ASSET OWNER determines that an EXTERNAL CASH FLOW may distort the return if the PORTFOLIO or TOTAL FUND is not valued and a sub-period return is not calculated. The FIRM or ASSET OWNER MUST define the amount in terms of the value of cash/asset flow or in terms of a percentage of the PORTFOLIO assets, COMPOSITE assets, or TOTAL FUND assets. The FIRM or ASSET OWNER MUST also determine if a LARGE CASH FLOW is a single EXTERNAL CASH FLOW or an aggregate of a number of EXTERNAL CASH FLOWS within a stated period.

LIMITED DISTRIBUTION POOLED FUND

Any POOLED FUND that is not a BROAD DISTRIBUTION POOLED FUND.

LIMITED PARTNER

An investor in a LIMITED PARTNERSHIP.

LIMITED PARTNERSHIP

The legal structure used by many PRIVATE MARKET INVESTMENT CLOSED-END POOLED FUNDS. LIMITED PARTNERSHIPS are usually FIXED LIFE investment vehicles. The GENERAL PARTNER manages the LIMITED PARTNERSHIP pursuant to the partnership agreement.

LINK

The method by which sub-period returns are geometrically combined to calculate the period return, or by which periodic returns are geometrically combined to calculate longer-period returns using the following formula:

$$\text{Period return} = [(1 + R_1) \times (1 + R_2) \ldots (1 + R_n)] - 1$$

where R_1, R_2 … R_n are the sub-period or periodic returns for sub-periods or periods 1 through n, respectively.

MATERIAL ERROR

An error in a GIPS COMPOSITE REPORT, GIPS POOLED FUND REPORT, or GIPS ASSET OWNER REPORT that MUST be corrected and disclosed in a corrected GIPS COMPOSITE REPORT, GIPS POOLED FUND REPORT, or GIPS ASSET OWNER REPORT.

MUST	A provision, task, or action that is mandatory or REQUIRED to be followed or performed. (See "REQUIRE/REQUIREMENT.")
MUST NOT	A task or action that is forbidden or prohibited.
NET-OF-FEES	For FIRMS, the GROSS-OF-FEES return reduced by INVESTMENT MANAGEMENT FEES. For ASSET OWNERS, the return that reflects the deduction of TRANSACTION COSTS, all fees and expenses for externally managed POOLED FUNDS, INVESTMENT MANAGEMENT FEES for externally managed SEGREGATED ACCOUNTS, and INVESTMENT MANAGEMENT COSTS.
OVERLAY EXPOSURE	The economic value for which a FIRM has investment management responsibility. OVERLAY EXPOSURE is the notional value of the OVERLAY STRATEGY being managed, the value of the underlying PORTFOLIOS being overlaid, or a specified target exposure.
OVERLAY STRATEGY	A strategy in which the management of a certain aspect of an investment strategy is carried out separately from the underlying PORTFOLIO. OVERLAY STRATEGIES are typically designed to either limit or maintain a specified risk exposure that is present in the underlying PORTFOLIO or to profit from a tactical view of the market by changing a PORTFOLIO's specified risk exposure.
OVERSIGHT BODY	Those who have direct oversight responsibility for TOTAL FUND assets and TOTAL ASSET OWNER ASSETS.
PERFORMANCE-BASED FEE	A type of INVESTMENT MANAGEMENT FEE that is typically based on the PORTFOLIO's performance on an absolute basis or relative to a BENCHMARK or other reference point.
PERFORMANCE EXAMINATION	A process by which an independent verifier conducts testing of a specific COMPOSITE, POOLED FUND, or TOTAL FUND, in accordance with the REQUIRED PERFORMANCE EXAMINATION procedures of the GIPS standards.
PERFORMANCE EXAMINATION REPORT	A report issued by an independent verifier after a PERFORMANCE EXAMINATION has been performed.
PERFORMANCE-RELATED INFORMATION	Includes: • Information expressed in terms of investment return and risk. • Other information and input data that directly relate to the calculation of investment return and risk (e.g., PORTFOLIO holdings), as well as information derived from investment return and risk input data (e.g., performance contribution or attribution).

(continued)

POOLED FUND	A fund whose ownership interests may be held by more than one investor.
POOLED FUND DESCRIPTION	General information regarding the investment mandate, objective, or strategy of the POOLED FUND. The POOLED FUND DESCRIPTION MUST include enough information to allow a PROSPECTIVE INVESTOR to understand the key characteristics of the POOLED FUND'S investment mandate, objective, or strategy, including: • The material risks of the POOLED FUND'S strategy. • How leverage, derivatives, and short positions may be used, if they are a material part of the strategy. • If ILLIQUID INVESTMENTS are a material part of the strategy.
POOLED FUND GROSS RETURN	The return on investments reduced by any TRANSACTION COSTS.
POOLED FUND NET RETURN	The POOLED FUND GROSS RETURN reduced by all fees and costs, including INVESTMENT MANAGEMENT FEES, ADMINISTRATIVE FEES, and other costs.
PORTFOLIO	For FIRMS, an individually managed group of investments. A PORTFOLIO may be a SEGREGATED ACCOUNT or a POOLED FUND, including assets managed by a SUB-ADVISOR for which the FIRM has discretion over the selection of the SUB-ADVISOR. For ASSET OWNERS, an account representing one of the strategies in or components of the ASSET OWNER'S TOTAL FUND, including assets managed by EXTERNAL MANAGERS for which the ASSET OWNER has discretion over the selection of the EXTERNAL MANAGER.
PRIVATE EQUITY	Investment strategies include, but are not limited to, venture capital, leveraged buyouts, consolidations, mezzanine and distressed debt investments, and a variety of hybrids, such as venture leasing and venture factoring.
PRIVATE MARKET INVESTMENTS	Includes real assets (e.g., REAL ESTATE and infrastructure), PRIVATE EQUITY, and similar investments that are illiquid, not publicly traded, and not traded on an exchange.
PROSPECTIVE CLIENT	Any person or entity that has expressed interest in one of the FIRM'S COMPOSITE strategies and qualifies to invest in the COMPOSITE. Existing clients may also qualify as PROSPECTIVE CLIENTS for any COMPOSITE strategy that differs from their current investment strategy. Investment consultants and other third parties are included as PROSPECTIVE CLIENTS if they represent investors that qualify as PROSPECTIVE CLIENTS.

PROSPECTIVE INVESTOR	Any person or entity that has expressed interest in one of the FIRM's POOLED FUNDS and qualifies to invest in the POOLED FUND. Existing POOLED FUND investors may also qualify as PROSPECTIVE INVESTORS for any POOLED FUND that differs from their current POOLED FUND. Investment consultants and other third parties are included as PROSPECTIVE INVESTORS if they represent investors that qualify as PROSPECTIVE INVESTORS.
REAL ESTATE	REAL ESTATE includes wholly owned or partially owned: • Investments in land, including products grown from the land (e.g., timber or crops). • Buildings under development, completed buildings, and other structures or improvements. • Equity-oriented debt (e.g., participating mortgage loans). • Private interest in a property for which some portion of the return to the investor at the time of investment relates to the performance of the underlying REAL ESTATE.
RECOMMEND/ RECOMMENDATION	A suggested provision, task, or action that SHOULD be followed or performed. A RECOMMENDATION is considered to be best practice but is not a REQUIREMENT. (See "SHOULD.")
REQUIRE/REQUIREMENT	A provision, task, or action that MUST be followed or performed.
SEGREGATED ACCOUNT	For FIRMS, a PORTFOLIO owned by a single client. For ASSET OWNERS, a PORTFOLIO managed by an EXTERNAL MANAGER.
SHOULD	A provision, task, or action that is RECOMMENDED to be followed or performed and is considered to be best practice but is not REQUIRED.
SIGNIFICANT CASH FLOW	The level at which the FIRM determines that one or more client-directed EXTERNAL CASH FLOWS may temporarily prevent the FIRM from implementing the COMPOSITE strategy. The cash flow may be defined by the FIRM as a single flow or an aggregate of a number of flows within a stated period. The measure of significance MUST be determined as either a specific monetary amount (e.g., €50,000,000) or a percentage of PORTFOLIO assets (based on the most recent valuation), and no other criteria, such as the effect of the cash flow or the number of PORTFOLIOS in the COMPOSITE, may be considered. Transfers of assets between asset classes within a PORTFOLIO or FIRM-initiated cash flows MUST NOT be considered SIGNIFICANT CASH FLOWS.

(continued)

SUB-ADVISOR	A third-party investment manager hired by the FIRM to manage some or all of the assets for which a FIRM has investment management responsibility. May also be referred to as a sub-manager or third-party investment manager.
SUPPLEMENTAL INFORMATION	Any PERFORMANCE-RELATED INFORMATION included as part of a GIPS COMPOSITE REPORT, GIPS POOLED FUND REPORT, or GIPS ASSET OWNER REPORT that supplements or enhances the REQUIREMENTS and/or RECOMMENDATIONS of the GIPS standards.
TOTAL ASSET OWNER ASSETS	All discretionary and non-discretionary assets for which an ASSET OWNER has investment management responsibility. TOTAL ASSET OWNER ASSETS include assets assigned to an EXTERNAL MANAGER provided the ASSET OWNER has discretion over the selection of the EXTERNAL MANAGER.
TOTAL FIRM ASSETS	All discretionary and non-discretionary assets for which a FIRM has investment management responsibility. TOTAL FIRM ASSETS include assets assigned to a SUB-ADVISOR provided the FIRM has discretion over the selection of the SUB-ADVISOR.
TOTAL FUND	A pool of assets managed by an ASSET OWNER according to a specific investment mandate, which is typically composed of multiple asset classes. The TOTAL FUND usually consists of underlying PORTFOLIOS, each representing one of the strategies used to achieve the ASSET OWNER's investment mandate.
TOTAL POOLED FUND FEES	All fees and expenses charged to the POOLED FUND, including but not limited to INVESTMENT MANAGEMENT FEES and ADMINISTRATIVE FEES.
TOTAL RETURN	The rate of return that includes the realized and unrealized gains and losses plus income for the measurement period.
TRANSACTION COSTS	The costs of buying or selling investments. These costs typically take the form of brokerage commissions, exchange fees and/or taxes, and/or bid–offer spreads from either internal or external brokers. Custodial fees charged per transaction SHOULD be considered CUSTODY FEES and not TRANSACTION COSTS. For REAL ESTATE, PRIVATE EQUITY, and other PRIVATE MARKET INVESTMENTS, TRANSACTION COSTS include all legal, financial, advisory, and investment banking fees related to buying, selling, restructuring, and/or recapitalizing investments but do not include dead deal costs.

VERIFICATION	A process by which an independent verifier conducts testing of a FIRM on a FIRM-wide basis, or an ASSET OWNER on an ASSET OWNER–wide basis, in accordance with the REQUIRED VERIFICATION procedures of the GIPS standards.
VERIFICATION REPORT	A report issued by an independent verifier after a VERIFICATION has been performed.

APPENDIX A: SAMPLE INDEPENDENT VERIFIER'S VERIFICATION REPORT

Independent Verifier's Verification Report

Buku Management
20 Squirrel Lane
Waggle, WA 55555

We have verified whether Buku Management (the Firm) has, for the periods from 1 January 2015 through 31 December 2020, established policies and procedures for complying with the Global Investment Performance Standards (GIPS®) related to composite and pooled fund maintenance and the calculation, presentation, and distribution of performance that are designed in compliance with the GIPS standards, as well as whether these policies and procedures have been implemented on a firm-wide basis. GIPS® is a registered trademark of CFA Institute. CFA Institute does not endorse or promote this organization, nor does it warrant the accuracy or quality of the content contained herein.

The Firm's management is responsible for its claim of compliance with the GIPS standards and the design and implementation of its policies and procedures. Our responsibilities are to be independent from the Firm and to express an opinion based on our verification. We conducted this verification in accordance with the required verification procedures of the GIPS standards, which includes testing performed on a sample basis. We also conducted such other procedures as we considered necessary in the circumstances.

In our opinion, for the periods from 1 January 2015 through 31 December 2020, the Firm's policies and procedures for complying with the GIPS standards related to composite and pooled fund maintenance, as well as the calculation, presentation, and distribution of performance, have been, in all material respects:

- Designed in compliance with the GIPS standards, and
- Implemented on a firm-wide basis.

This report does not relate to or provide assurance on any specific performance report of the Firm or on the operating effectiveness of the Firm's controls or policies and procedures for complying with the GIPS standards.

ABC Verifier
14 May 2021

APPENDIX B: SAMPLE INDEPENDENT VERIFIER'S PERFORMANCE EXAMINATION REPORT

Independent Verifier's Performance Examination Report

Buku Management
20 Squirrel Lane
Waggle, WA 55555

We have verified whether Buku Management (the Firm) has, for the periods from 1 January 2015 through 31 December 2020, established policies and procedures for complying with the Global Investment Performance Standards (GIPS®)[1] related to composite and pooled fund maintenance and the calculation, presentation, and distribution of performance that are designed in compliance with the GIPS standards, as well as whether these policies and procedures have been implemented on a firm-wide basis. We have also examined the Firm's Aggressive Growth Composite for the periods 1 January 2018 through 31 December 2020.

The Firm's management is responsible for its claim of compliance with the GIPS standards, the design and implementation of its policies and procedures, and for the accompanying Aggressive Growth Composite's GIPS composite report. Our responsibilities are to be independent from the Firm and to express an opinion based on our verification and performance examination. We conducted this verification and performance examination in accordance with the required verification and performance examination procedures of the GIPS standards, which includes testing performed on a sample basis. We also conducted such other procedures as we considered necessary in the circumstances.

In our opinion, for the periods from 1 January 2015 through 31 December 2020, the Firm's policies and procedures for complying with the GIPS standards related to composite and pooled fund maintenance, as well as the calculation, presentation, and distribution of performance, have been, in all material respects:

- Designed in compliance with the GIPS standards, and
- Implemented on a firm-wide basis.

[1] GIPS® is a registered trademark of CFA Institute. CFA Institute does not endorse or promote this organization, nor does it warrant the accuracy or quality of the content contained herein.

Also, in our opinion, the Firm has, in all material respects:

- Constructed the Aggressive Growth Composite and calculated the Aggressive Growth Composite's performance for the periods from 1 January 2018 through 31 December 2020 in compliance with the GIPS standards, and
- Prepared and presented the accompanying Aggressive Growth Composite's GIPS composite report for the periods from 1 January 2018 through 31 December 2020 in compliance with the GIPS standards.

We have not been engaged to examine, and did not examine, the Firm's Aggressive Growth Composite for any periods prior to 1 January 2018 and, accordingly, we express no opinion on the GIPS composite report of the Firm's Aggressive Growth Composite for any periods prior to 1 January 2018.

This report does not relate to or provide assurance on any specific performance report of the Firm other than the Firm's accompanying Aggressive Growth Composite's GIPS composite report, or on the operating effectiveness of the Firm's controls or policies and procedures for complying with the GIPS standards.

XYZ Verifier
14 May 2021

Made in United States
North Haven, CT
05 November 2026

21771555R10030